MACHINES ON THE MOVE

BUSES

by Natalie Deniston

TABLE OF CONTENTS

Tadpole Books, an imprint of Jump! Library by FlutterBee

tadpole books

WORDS TO KNOW

bus stop

cord

doors

ride

sign

waits

BUSES

She waits at a bus stop.

STOP ID
6489
FAIRFAX CONNECTOR
BusTracker

A bus comes.

Where will it go?

A sign says.

door

The doors open.

We ride.

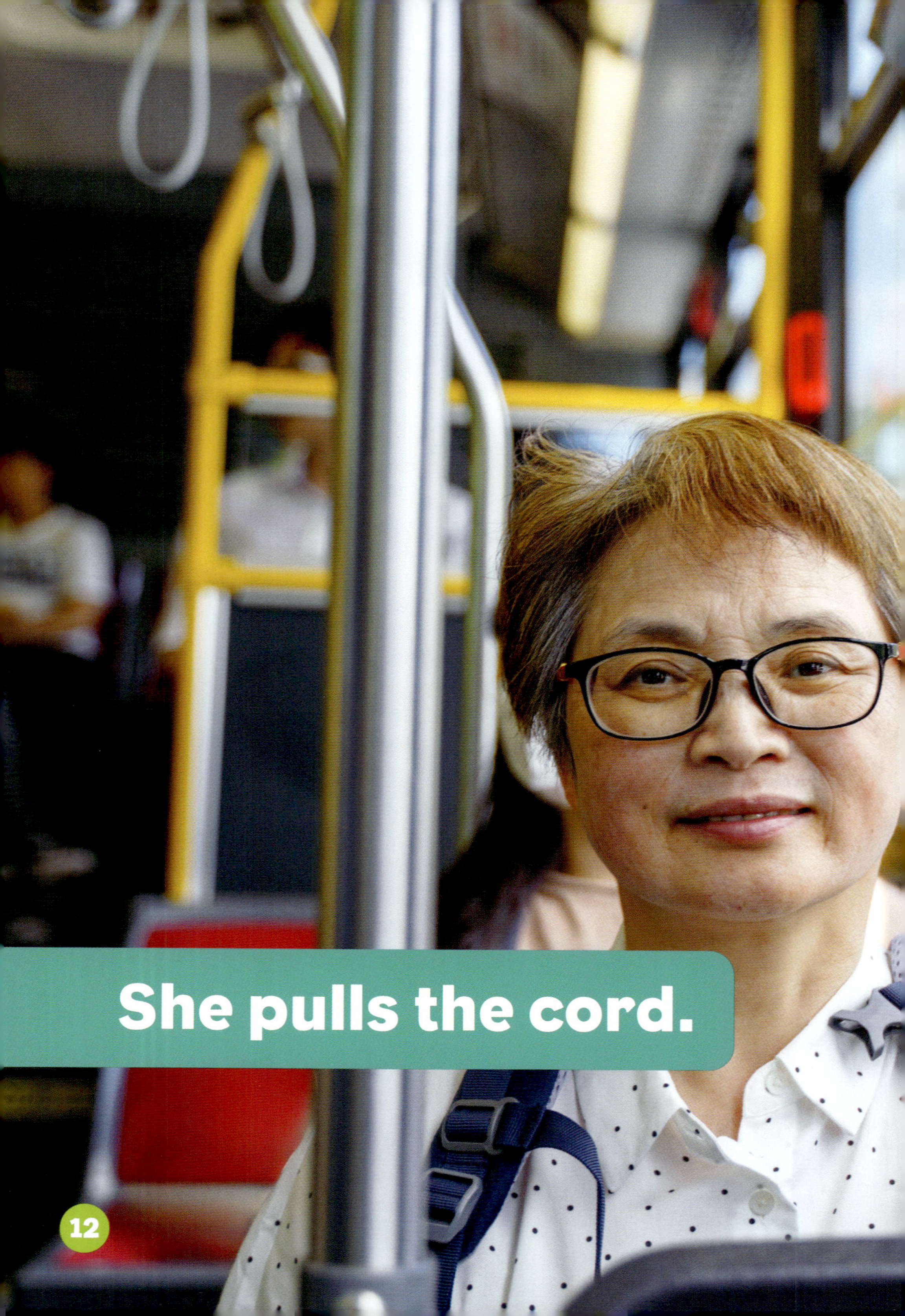
She pulls the cord.

The bus stops!

11

Thank you!

LET'S REVIEW!

Buses take people places. Where is this bus going? How do you know?

INDEX